Symbols of Freedom

The Pledge of Allegiance

Lola Schaefer

Heinemann Library
Chicago, Illinois

© 2002 Reed Educational & Professional Publishing
Published by Heinemann Library,
an imprint of Reed Educational & Professional Publishing,
Chicago, IL

Customer Service 888-454-2279

Visit our website at www.heinemannlibrary.com

Designed by Depke Design
Printed and bound at Lake Book Manufacturing

06 05
10 9 8 7 6 5 4

Library of Congress Cataloging-in-Publication Data
Schaefer, Lola M., 1950-
      The Pledge of Allegiance / Lola M. Schaefer.
          p. cm. -- (Symbols of Freedom)
      Includes bibliographical references and index.
      ISBN 1-58810-177-0
      1. Bellamy, Francis. Pledge of allegiance to the flag--Juvenile
literature. 2. Flags--United States--Juvenile literature. [1. Pledge of
Allegiance. 2. Flags--United States.] I. Title. II. Series.
      JC346 .S33 2001
      323.6'5'0973--dc21
                                      2001001632
Acknowledgments
The author and publishers are grateful to the following for permission to reproduce copyright material:
Cover photograph: Shelly Katz/TimePix
pp. 4, 10, 15, 17 Michael Brosilow/Heinemann Library; pp. 5, 6 Corbis; p. 7 Mary Kate Denny/PictureQuest; p. 8
Tony Freeman/PhotoEdit/PictureQuest; p. 9 Morton Beebe, S.F./Corbis; p. 11 James Marshall/Corbis; p. 12
PhotoDisc; p. 13 Joe Sohm, Chromosohm/Stock Connection/PictureQuest; pp. 18, 21 The Rome Historical Society;
p. 19 Boston Public Library/Rare Book Department. Courtesy of the Trustees; p. 20 Oscar White/Corbis; p. 23
Watertown Free Public Library; p. 24 Library and Archives, The American Legion National Headquarters,
Indianapolis, Indiana; p. 25 Nathan Benn/Stock, Boston/PictureQuest; p. 26 Bettman/Corbis; p. 27 Yogi,
Inc./Corbis; p. 29 AFP/Corbis

Special thanks to Stockton School.

Every effort has been made to contact copyright holders of any material reproduced in this book.
Any omissions will be rectified in subsequent printings if notice is given to the publisher.

Some words are shown in bold, **like this.**
You can find out what they mean by looking
in the glossary.

Contents

The Pledge of Allegiance

These children are saying the Pledge of **Allegiance.** Many Americans say the pledge every day.

The Pledge of Allegiance **honors** the United States flag. The flag is a **symbol** of our country. It stands for the freedoms of all Americans.

What Is the Pledge?

The pledge is a promise to the United States. The words of the pledge remind people of the **rights** they have as Americans.

The Pledge of **Allegiance** is one way to show **patriotism** in public. It lets others know that you respect the flag and care about the United States.

Who Says the Pledge?

All United States **citizens** can say the Pledge of **Allegiance.** Children and adults sometimes say the pledge at sports events.

Immigrants become United States citizens in a special **ceremony.** The people promise to be **loyal** to the United States. At that ceremony, they may say the Pledge of Allegiance.

Schools and Meetings

Children say the Pledge of **Allegiance** at school. This is a time when they can think about their country. They think about how they can be good **citizens**.

Boy Scout and Girl Scout meetings begin with the pledge. People also say the pledge at **community** meetings.

How People Say the Pledge

Americans face the United States flag as they say the Pledge of **Allegiance.** They place their right hands over their hearts.

People in the **armed forces salute** the flag during the Pledge of Allegiance. They stand silently while people say the pledge out loud.

What the Pledge of Allegiance Means

I pledge **allegiance** *to the flag of the United States of America. . .*

To pledge means to make a promise.
Allegiance means "faithful."
With these words, a person promises to stay **loyal** to the United States.

. . .and to the Republic for which it stands. . .

A republic is the kind of **government** in the United States. In a republic, people vote for their leaders.

One Nation under God, indivisible. . .

"One nation" means that all 50 states together make one United States. "Indivisible" means that the country cannot be split apart by war or groups of people.

. . .with liberty and justice for all.

Liberty is another word for freedom. All Americans have the same freedoms. "Justice for all" means that the laws in the United States are the same for every person. Everyone must be treated fairly.

Who Wrote the Pledge of Allegiance?

Francis Bellamy wrote the first Pledge of **Allegiance.** It was printed in a magazine for children in September, 1892.

The magazine was called *The Youth's Companion*. In the 1890s, more than 480 thousand children read this magazine.

The First Pledge of Allegiance

In 1892, President Benjamin Harrison made **Columbus Day** a national holiday. The first Pledge of **Allegiance** was one part of the Columbus Day celebration for children.

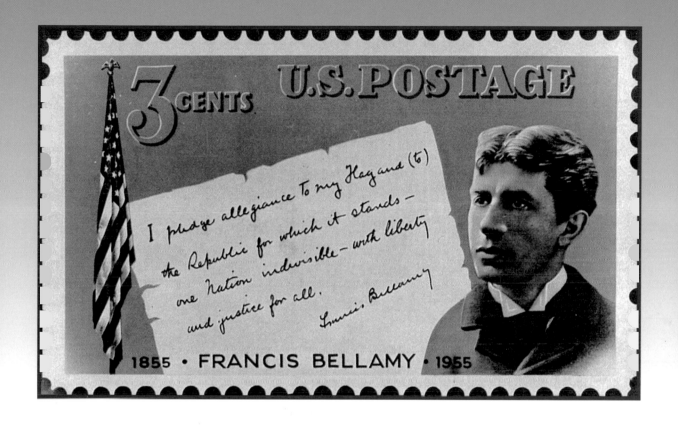

The first Pledge of Allegiance only had 23 words. This old stamp shows the pledge that Francis Bellamy wrote. It began with the words, "I pledge allegiance to my Flag."

School Celebration

Francis Bellamy and a friend from *The Youth's Companion* wrote a **Columbus Day** program for school children. It was called the "**Salute** to the Flag."

On Columbus Day in 1892, Francis Bellamy heard 6,000 children say the "Salute to the Flag" in Boston, Massachusetts. During this pledge, the children saluted the flag.

Changes to the Pledge

After **World War I,** a group of people met. Many of the men were **veterans.** They wanted to change the Pledge of **Allegiance.** The first words would be, "I pledge allegiance to the Flag of the United States of America."

This group also decided that people should put their right hands over their hearts during the pledge. People still say the pledge this way today.

Fifty Years Old

On **Columbus Day** in 1942, the Pledge of **Allegiance** was fifty years old. President Franklin Roosevelt made the pledge part of United States law.

Since that day, only the **government** can change or add words to the Pledge of Allegiance.

The Last Change

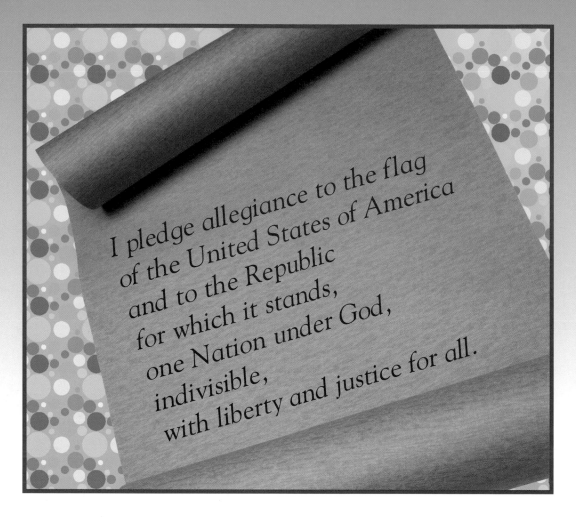

I pledge allegiance to the flag of the United States of America and to the Republic for which it stands, one Nation under God, indivisible, with liberty and justice for all.

In 1954, **Congress** added the words "under God" after the word "nation." That was the last change to the Pledge of **Allegiance.**

The Pledge of Allegiance is now more than 100 years old. Americans are proud to say these words again and again.

Fact File

The Pledge of Allegiance

★ More than 2 million schoolchildren in the United States said the first Pledge of **Allegiance** on **Columbus Day,** October 12, 1892.

★ In 1923, all United States public schools began leading their students in the Pledge of Allegiance at the beginning of each day.

★ No one has to say The Pledge of Allegiance. Some people do not say the pledge because of their **religious beliefs**.

★ On Flag Day, June 14, many Americans stop work or play at 7 P.M. Eastern Time and say the Pledge of Allegiance.

Glossary

allegiance faithful support for someone or something

armed forces all of the branches of the military, including the Army, Navy, Air Force, Marine Corps, and Coast Guard

ceremony gathering of people for an important event

citizen person who lives in a town, city, or country

Columbus Day holiday celebrated on the second Monday in October to remember the day in 1492 when Christopher Columbus landed in North America

community area where people live, work, and shop

Congress group of people in the United States government who decide what the laws will be

government people who rule or govern a country or state

honor to do something that shows great respect for someone or something

immigrant person who moves to a different country to live

liberty freedom to choose your work, your religion, and your friends

loyal faithful and true

patriotism person's love of his or her country

religious beliefs what a person believes about God

rights something someone deserves without having to ask for it, such as being treated fairly by everyone

salute to raise your right hand to your forehead as a sign of respect

symbol something that stands for an idea

veteran person who has fought in a war

World War I war fought in Europe between 1914 and 1918 in which America, Britain, France, and other countries fought against Germany

More Books to Read

Ansary, Tamim. *Columbus Day*. Chicago: Heinemann Library, 1999.

Kallen, Stuart A. *The Pledge of Allegiance*. Minneapolis: ABDO Publishing, 1994. An older reader can help you with this book.

Swanson, June. *I Pledge Allegiance*. Minneapolis: Lerner, 1990.

Index